Chrysanthemums

CHRYSANTHEMUM FRED SHOESMITH

A new incurving decorative, white with creamy centre, which received a First-Class Certificate in 1953.

AMATEUR GARDENING PICTURE BOOK NO 1

Chrysanthemums

EDITED BY A. G. L. HELLYER, F.L.S., A.H.R.H.S.

W. H. & L. COLLINGRIDGE LIMITED LONDON

FIRST PUBLISHED IN 1954

*The Amateur Gardening Picture Books
are published by
W. H. & L. Collingridge Limited
2-10 Tavistock Street London W.C.2
and printed and bound in England by
Vandyck Printers Bristol and London
and James Burn & Co. Limited
London and Esher*

© *W. H. & L. Collingridge Ltd.,* 1954
Third impression 1958

UNIFORM WITH THIS BOOK

No. 2   Roses
No. 3   Tomatoes
No. 4   Plant Propagation
No. 5   Herbaceous Borders
No. 6   Garden Making (*Double Size*)
No. 7   Dahlias
No. 8   Indoor Plants
No. 9   Pruning
No. 10   Greenhouse Management

Contents

The Time to Start   9

Striking Cuttings   11

Propagating Outdoor Varieties   16

Potting On   22

Potting Indoor Types   25

Bought Plants   26

Repotting Outdoor Varieties   28

Final Potting of Indoor Varieties   29

Planting Outdoor Varieties   32

Summer Quarters   36

Stopping   37

Shading Outdoor Blooms   43

Housing Indoor Varieties   45

Cutting Blooms   47

Transporting Blooms   48

Staging Blooms   51

Raising New Varieties   53

Pests and Diseases   54

Some Types of Chrysanthemum   56

Chrysanthemums

The chrysanthemum has been well named 'The Queen of Autumn Flowers' and the growing membership of the National Chrysanthemum Society and its affiliated Societies, the attendance at the great shows and the exhibits at the shows of hundreds of local horticultural societies, all testify to the popularity of a plant which with its wide range of form and colouring can offer something to everyone.

It is true that anyone can grow chrysanthemums, probably without a great deal of trouble provided certain simple basic rules are followed. Certainly hundreds of thousands of plants are sent out each year by nurserymen and scores of thousands are propagated by amateurs, often with the minimum of equipment, and often without the aid of a heated greenhouse.

Many books have been written on chrysanthemum culture and it is certainly the man who knows what he is doing and why he is doing it and can, therefore, give his plants just that little extra, who produces blooms that are better than those of his neighbours, and who wins prizes at his local shows or at the bigger shows.

Harold Alston, a reflexed decorative, one of the brightest of all red chrysanthemums.

A good display of outdoor chrysanthemums

Not everyone wants to exhibit his blooms ; many gardeners are content to produce good blooms for their own delight and for decorating their homes. But I have known many in my time who, starting off in a modest way with a few plants, given to them by friends or bought from a nurseryman, grow better and better blooms as they gain experience, and eventually exhibit successfully.

In this book, therefore, I have described every stage in the culture of chrysanthemums so that it will be of value to the beginner and the more experienced gardener, to the would-be exhibitor and to the gardener who simply wants to grow good blooms for home decoration.

There are certain differences between the cultivation of indoor chrysanthemums and that of outdoor varieties. Much of the basic culture is the same but where necessary I have diverged to indicate the special points which arise from time to time. All aspects of the cultivation of both types are described in detail, and I have taken the reader step by step through all the important operations, describing each stage with the aid of the many illustrations.

Those who are interested in propagating their own plants by means of cuttings should read straight on, but those who for various reasons prefer to buy their plants as rooted cuttings from a nursery should start at page 26 where I have described the treatment these young plants require when they are received.

THE TIME TO START

Perhaps the best point at which to start the story of chrysanthemums culture is that at which the grower must think of propagating his plants ready for the coming season. Cuttings of many varieties are rooted in January so that it is also a convenient starting point in time. This book then starts at the beginning of the year, with the beginning of all chrysanthemum culture—the rooting of cuttings.

I propose to deal at length with the striking of cuttings because it is by far the best way of propagating chrysanthemums. It is, of course, possible to propagate by dividing the old stools into pieces and planting these, and also by detaching small shoots from the stool each bearing its complement of roots. But neither of these methods is. as reliable as taking cuttings, especially where plants of first-class quality are required.

When outdoor plants have finished flowering in the autumn or early winter they should be cut down to within a few inches of the ground, carefully labelled, lifted, placed in boxes and covered with compost. The boxes are then placed in their winter quarters in a frame as seen below. With indoor varieties the procedure is essentially the same, except that the old stools are kept in the greenhouse. They may be left in their pots but it is better to turn them out into boxes or beds of fresh soil.

Whether the plants are inside the greenhouse or in frames the compost should be kept just moist to ensure that the roots do not dry out. Some air should be allowed, except in frosty weather, to maintain a buoyant atmosphere.

In frosty weather protection should be provided for the frames. In the illustration roofing felt has been spread over the lights, but mats or sacks will do as well. Except during periods of frost the lights should be left a little open. To prevent slugs damaging the young shoots trap them with crushed metaldehyde mixed with bran. Against woodlice a 5% DDT dust is an effective remedy.

Below, the stools, bedded out on the greenhouse staging have produced plenty of new growth suitable for cuttings.

STRIKING CUTTINGS

Cuttings of ordinary outdoor varieties are taken in February and March, while those of indoor varieties are taken from mid-November (e.g. Majestic which needs a long season of growth) to early March (for Decorative and Single Indoor types).

When varieties which normally flower in October are required to bloom in September for early shows, cuttings are taken in January from new growths springing from the old growths. With these varieties the basal growths are not removed in October as new roots and shoots would not form in time.

The stool is lifted from its box taking care not to damage the young growths. On the right it can be seen that most of the young growths arise from the roots. These are the best growths for cuttings except from the mid-season varieties mentioned above, or varieties which are backward in forming new shoots, when stem growths must be taken.

11

Before taking the cuttings a suitable rooting compost should be prepared. John Innes seed compost is often used and is made by mixing together 2 parts of sterilized loam, 1 part of moist granulated peat and 1 part of coarse, sharp sand. To each bushel is added $\frac{3}{4}$ oz. of carbonate of lime and $1\frac{1}{2}$ oz. superphosphate. A bushel is contained in a box $22 \times 10 \times 10$ in. Instead of lifting the stools from their boxes the shoots may be cut off as shown. This is a better method where there is a shortage of stock plants as the roots will then produce further growths which can be taken as cuttings later.

The best cuttings are obtained from short sturdy shoots. That on the right in the top photograph is a typical example of a suitable shoot while that on the left is a little too long to give the best results. These short sturdy growths are obtained by growing the stools in a steady, buoyant atmosphere, not too warm and not too moist, opening the ventilators in the greenhouse or the frame on the side opposite to that which the wind is blowing, on all possible occasions.

In the centre illustration the shoot is being severed from the stool with a sharp knife, below a leaf joint. The selected cuttings should be from 2 to $2\frac{1}{2}$ inches long and they must be cut off cleanly—ragged or torn stems provide entry points for the spores of fungal diseases.

In the bottom picture on the opposite page is shown the first important stage in the preparation of the cuttings for insertion. The cutting is held gently in the fingers and the lower leaves pulled off carefully upwards, never downwards, as this may tear the stem.

The next operation is to trim the foot of the cutting immediately below a leaf joint. Again it is essential that this cut should be made cleanly and an old, clean razor blade is the ideal tool. A thick sheet of glass or a glazed tile provides a steady, hard surface for trimming the shoots on. If the job is attempted on a rough surface such as the potting bench then it is possible that the cut will not be a clean one.

The picture below shows the prepared cutting.

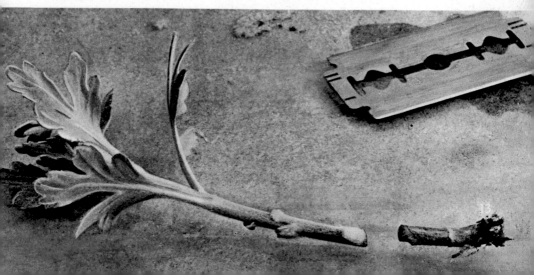

Cuttings may be rooted in pots as shown here, or in boxes. Sharp sand is sprinkled on the surface of the compost as shown in the top picture. Some will fall to the bottom of the hole when cuttings are inserted enabling them to root more readily. Before insertion the cuttings are immersed in a weak nicotine solution to destroy any greenfly. Although it is not essential, the cut surfaces of the cuttings may be dipped in one of the proprietary hormone rooting powders as shown on the bottom right.

Five or six cuttings are inserted round the edge of a 3-inch pot, using a small dibber, and are well firmed. When completed the pots should be given a thorough watering which, apart from an occasional fine spray to counteract undue flagging, should suffice until roots have formed. Some flagging is inevitable and in the bottom picture the cuttings on the left have been inserted six days previously while those on the right have been in a fortnight and have recovered. This recovery is usually a sign that rooting has started.

15

When the pots have been well watered they should be placed in a propagating frame on the greenhouse staging or inside a garden frame. Bottom heat will help rooting but is not essential, but an air temperature of 55° to 60° must be maintained inside the propagating frame. Soil-warming wires have been used to provide bottom heat in the frame above. The pots were bedded in peat which has been scraped away to show the low-voltage wires leading to the mains transformer.

PROPAGATING OUTDOOR VARIETIES

Cuttings of outdoor or early-flowering varieties are usually rooted in boxes in February or March according to variety or season. Below, the John Innes compost described earlier is being mixed.

Use fairly deep boxes. If the drainage slits in the bottom are too narrow enlarge them with a penknife. A layer of coarse peat is put in the bottom of the box, followed by the compost.

Another method suitable for stools grown in a cold frame is to insert cuttings in a frame in mid-February. On the base of the frame spread a 3-inch layer of fine ashes. On this spread a layer of compost consisting of 5 parts of finely sieved loam and 1 of red ash (as used on hard tennis courts). Finish off with a $\frac{1}{2}$-inch layer of sharp sand. Water the bed a few days before inserting cuttings, and provide protection from frost.

The compost in the boxes is firmed with the fingers, making sure that the corners are filled properly. It is then pressed down gently with a firmer to give it a final firming, leaving a $1\frac{1}{2}$ inch space at the top of the box.

Finally a layer of sharp sand is sprinkled on the surface of the compost in the same way as when pots are used. The cuttings are then inserted in rows in the compost. Where only a few of a number of varieties are being propagated the different varieties are kept in separate rows each labelled with the name of the variety and the date of insertion, as shown below.

A small dibber is used to make the holes. The cuttings are set out evenly in rows, with labels at the end of each row. Note how in that part of the box in which cuttings have been inserted the sand has disappeared. It has trickled into the holes as they were made.

As mentioned earlier the cuttings should be firmed with the fingers when they are put in. This is most important as unless the base of the cutting rests firmly on the bottom of the hole and the compost is firmed round it rooting will be difficult, if not impossible. It is important, too, to see that cuttings are inserted to the correct depth. It is a mistake to insert them too deeply.

It is usual to root about 30 cuttings in a box of the normal seed box dimensions, i.e. $14\frac{1}{2} \times 8\frac{1}{2} \times 3$ inches. When all the cuttings have been inserted and properly firmed, give a final check over to see that the labels showing the name of the variety and the date of insertion are all in place at the ends of the rows. Then water the box from a can with a fine rose. This watering should be a good one because no more water should be required until the cuttings have rooted, in about three weeks. However, it is fatal to allow the boxes to dry out and if at any time the cuttings appear to be flagging unduly and the compost seems dry and crumbly then a light overhead spraying with a syringe should be given. But on no account over-water otherwise the cuttings will rot.

The boxes should now be covered with a sheet of glass to provide the warm moist atmosphere which is conducive to rooting. The boxes are placed on the greenhouse staging or on shelves as near to the light as possible. Condensation will cause drops of water to form on the underside of the sheet of glass and if these drops are allowed to fall on the cuttings it is possible that conditions suitable for the entry of fungal diseases will be set up. Accordingly the sheets of glass should be removed daily, wiped clean of moisture, reversed and put back. In the illustration cuttings are shown in various stages. Those below on the right are still rooting. Those on the bottom left have rooted and are being hardened off, while those above are ready for the next move into individual small pots.

POTTING ON

After about three weeks in the pots or boxes the cuttings should have made sufficient roots to allow them to be moved. Before this, however, they should be hardened off for a few days by giving them more ventilation. The two cuttings on the right have just started to make new roots while those on the left are several weeks old and have made good root systems, and are ready for their first move.

The cuttings are ready for potting into 3½-inch pots or deep boxes containing John Innes No. 1 potting compost, made up of 7 parts of sterilized loam, 3 parts of peat and 2 parts of coarse, sharp sand (all by volume). To every bushel add 1½ oz. each of superphosphate and hoof-and-horn meal and ¾ oz. each of sulphate of potash and carbonate of lime.

22

The best method is undoubtedly to transplant the cuttings individually to 3-inch or 3½-inch pots as in this way the plants suffer less check through root damage either at planting out time for outdoor types or at later potting stages for indoor types. If the plants have been rooted in boxes they are carefully removed with a small trowel, while if they have been rooted round the edges of small pots they are removed as shown in the top photograph. The fingers are carefully placed between the cuttings, the pot is reversed and its rim is tapped sharply on the edge of the potting bench. This will loosen the cuttings and the whole root ball can be removed from the pot without damage to the young roots.

In the centre illustration the new pot has been partly filled with the potting compost and the plant is placed in it as shown. More compost is added and gently firmed with the fingers avoiding undue pressure which may break off the young roots. More compost is added and firmed round the young plant until the compost is within ½ inch of the top of the pot. A final sharp tap on the bench will settle the surface of the compost.

Once again the plant should be dipped in a weak nicotine solution as shown in the bottom picture, to dispose of any pests, such as greenfly, which may have found a home on its stems or leaves. Too strong a solution will scorch the leaves and cause a check to growth. Note how the fingers are held over the surface of the compost while the plant is being dipped. This ensures that plant and compost are kept firmly in place.

23

After the rooted cuttings have been potted up they will require watering. The illustration above shows the correct method. Water is allowed to trickle gently into the pot from the spout of a watering-can and on no account allowed to rush out as the young plant and the compost will be greatly disturbed. The thumb can be used to control the flow of the water. The plants should then be returned to close, shaded conditions in the greenhouse for a day or two to allow them to recover. After that outdoor types can be moved into the frame again while indoor types can be placed on the staging near the light. In the frame the plants will need as much air and light as possible and lights should be put on only in exceptionally bad weather. In

the greenhouse ventilators should be kept open whenever possible. The plants will grow rapidly and on no account must the pots dry out. Space the pots out well so that plenty of air can circulate between them. Avoid checks of any kind but do not 'coddle' the plants. Indoor types are put out into the frame about the end of March and given as much air as possible after a few days of acclimatization.

POTTING INDOOR TYPES

Chrysanthemum composts should contain plenty of fibrous loam. This is obtained by stacking turves and leaving them for six months to rot down. Here a turf stack is being finished off. The turves are stacked in layers grass-side downwards and a good watering is given as each layer is completed. On acid soil carbonate of lime can be sprinkled on alternate layers at $\frac{1}{4}$ lb. per superficial yard. The stack should be built under an open-sided shed or if in the open it should be covered with a rain-proof tarpaulin in wet weather. It can be seen below how the turf rots down to a fibrous mass and this fibre is valuable in the potting composts, providing food for the plants and helping to keep the compost open and easily drained.

BOUGHT PLANTS

When the plants are bought by post from a nursery specializing in the sale of rooted cuttings they will arrive surrounded by fibre and securely packed in boxes. They should be lifted out of the box with great care not to disturb the ball of soil and young roots, and potted or planted out in boxes at once.

To ensure adequate drainage the pots should be well crocked. First of all a large piece of crock is put in concave side downwards covering the drainage hole in the pot. Then a good layer of smaller crocks is put in followed by a layer of rough peat or coarse parts of the compost.

During April the indoor types will require repotting into 5- or 6-inch pots according to the root system. The plant on the left is not yet ready for the roots have not yet developed sufficiently—repotting is necessary when the roots have taken full possession of the soil ball but have not become a tangled mass. For this second potting John Innes potting compost No. 2 is suitable. The ingredients are as for J.I.P. 1, described on page 22 but with double the amount of base fertilizer and chalk or carbonate of lime. Alternatively a good well-tried compost consists of 4 buckets of fibrous loam, 1 bucket of leaf-mould or peat, ½ bucket of coarse sand, 2 3-inch potfuls of bone flour and a good sprinkling of lime, plus 1 bucket of well-rotted manure.

In this series of photographs the operation of repotting is clearly depicted. The 5- or 6-inch pot has been crocked and filled to one-third its depth with fresh compost. The young plant, knocked out of its pot as described earlier, is placed in the centre of the new pot on the compost and held in place with one hand while compost is put round it with the other hand. It is gently firmed with the fingers and thumbs, particularly near the stem of the plant as shown below. Some growers use a small wooden rammer but the pressure of the fingers and thumbs is sufficient at this stage, combined with several taps of the pot on the bench to shake the compost down well. The new soil should not be too moist. At this stage a short cane can be inserted well away from the old root ball and the plant looped loosely to it. Take care to leave sufficient space at the top of the pot for watering.

REPOTTING OUTDOOR VARIETIES

If cuttings of outdoor varieties are not rooted until February or March, they can stay in the frame, once they have been potted into 3½-inch pots, until they can be planted out in the open ground. If, however, an earlier start was made and cuttings were rooted in January, by late March they will have become pot-bound and starved in the 3½-inch pots. This will result in a check to growth so that they should be potted on before this happens into 5- or 6-inch pots as shown on this page. Use J.I.P. Compost No. 2 or No. 3, (the latter has three times the amount of added fertilizer and carbonate of lime as J.I.P. 1 described on page 22 but the amounts of loam, peat and sand are the same). Note the label in position.

FINAL POTTING OF INDOOR VARIETIES

Between mid-May and early June the indoor varieties will need final potting and on the thoroughness with which this is done depends much of the future success. The actual date will be determined by the needs of the individual plant. It is a mistake to give too large a pot and where rooting is weak or the cutting was rooted later the 8-inch size may be adequate, but for those with a strong root system use the larger size up to 10-inch.

The final pot is crocked in the usual way using crocks sterilized with boiling water. Compost (described on the next page) is well pressed down to such a level as will leave the surface of the old soil ball about 3 inches below the rim of the pot.

For this final potting the J.I.P. 3 or 4 may be used (i.e. standard amounts of loam, peat and sand, but either three or four times the amounts of added fertilizer and carbonate of lime). A revised formula has been used with success : 8 parts of loam, $2\frac{1}{2}$ parts of peat and $1\frac{1}{2}$ parts of sand (all by bulk). A traditional compost consists of 4 buckets of loam, 1 of peat or leaf-mould, 1 of rotted manure, $\frac{1}{2}$ bucket each of wood ash and sand, a 6-inch pot each of soot, bonemeal and a base fertilizer such as Clay's or Bentley's, and a 4-inch pot of lime. This should be mixed a week or so before use, kept in a dry place, and turned occasionally. It must not be used if wet or sticky.

The plant is watered the day before it is to be repotted. It is turned out of its old pot and the root ball is stood centrally on a slight mound in the new pot as compost is added.

This potting must be fairly firm and a wooden rammer is used as shown. Every inch or so of the compost is firmed to obtain an even consistency throughout the pot. When you have finished the label should need a firm thumb pressure to drive it home. Keep the rammer close to the pot sides to avoid damaging the roots. Leave 3 inches at the top of the pot to allow for watering and subsequent top dressings. Insert a cane of suitable height well away from the old soil ball and loop the plant securely to it.

Alternatively, at this stage instead of one supporting cane being used, two may be inserted on opposite sides of the pot slanting slightly away from the plant, as shown on the right. The height of these canes may vary according to the usual height of the variety, but they are usually between 4 and 6 feet tall. The plant is supported by ties between the canes. These canes will be used later to support the stems as the plants are disbudded.

On the left is shown diagrammatically the use of a wire framework for training specimen plants. The centre stem of the plant is supported on a stout stake and the wires are fixed to this and to two stout stakes at right angles to each other placed across the top of the pot and fixed to the centre stake. The growths are tied in to these wires as the plant develops and final arrangement of the stems should hide every trace of the wire.

PLANTING OUTDOOR VARIETIES

Early in May, depending on the weather, early flowering chrysanthemums can be planted out. The ground, dug over and manured in the autumn should be dressed with a good general fertilizer at the rate of 3 oz. to the square yard, dug into the top 4 or 5 inches. The soil is then levelled off. On the right a simple planting plan is given which shows that plants should be planted 18 inches apart each way, in double rows, with a 2½ ft. pathway between the double rows. In this way the plants can be reached without undue trampling of the soil. Below, a plant is being knocked out of its pot ready for planting.

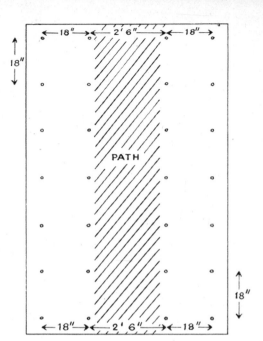

The ground should be raked and levelled and a line stretched across the plot to make the first row. Canes 2 ft. long are then pushed in along the line 18 inches apart. Make the planting holes as near to the stakes as possible, big enough to accommodate the root base, and deep enough to allow the roots to be covered $\frac{1}{2}$ inch deeper than when in pots.

Always use a trowel for making the holes. It is a good plan to use a board for kneeling on as shown, to avoid the necessity for treading on the soil.

The plant is held in position and fine soil filled in round the roots and pressed in firmly with the handle of the trowel. If the soil is heavy a quantity of fine, dry sifted soil should be prepared beforehand.

Young chrysanthemum plants require firm planting (remember how in the final potting of indoor varieties a wooden rammer is used), and after more soil is put round them they should be given a final firming with the ball of the foot.

The plant is then tied to the short cane as shown. It will require to be tied to this cane once more just before it is stopped or is about to break naturally.

It is a good plan to stretch black cotton from one stake to the next all over the plot to frighten off sparrows as these are liable to nip out the tops of the young plants.

If dry soil used for planting then the plants should be well watered after planting to avoid any check to growth.

About mid-June the plants will benefit from a mulch of stable manure, peat, compost, grass cuttings or straw. The whole plot should be hoed and then the mulch put down about 2 inches thick. A 2 cwt. bale of peat is sufficient for 150 plants.

Make a practice of spraying the plants once a week with an insecticide. If alternate applications of BHC and nicotine with the addition of DDT or HETP are given, a good control of aphides (greenfly, blackfly, plant lice), leaf miners, earwigs, capsid bugs, frog and leaf hoppers, woodlice and caterpillars. A combined BHC and Thiram spray will also control the fungal diseases rust and powdery mildew. Always spray thoroughly, drenching the undersides of the leaves as well as the tops. Slugs and snails can be dealt with by placing small heaps of powdered metaldehyde and bran at intervals between the plants or by using one of the proprietary slug baits.

SUMMER QUARTERS

By the end of June indoor varieties should be out on the standing grounds. Choose a spot sheltered from high winds but open to as much light and air as possible. Stand the pots on ashes, bricks, slates, boards or anything which will prevent worms from entering the pots. Wires stretched tightly between posts and the canes tied to them will prevent wind damage. A more elaborate method is shown on the left.

Growth will be rapid and more water will be needed. Go over the plants daily tapping the pots to see whether water is required (a hollow ring means that water is required, a dull sound means that none is needed immediately). Give plenty of water, not just a trickle. A light overhead spray is beneficial in hot weather.

About five weeks after potting start feeding at frequent intervals with a proprietary feed according to the manufacturer's directions, beginning with weak doses.

If blooms of exhibition quality are not required the plants may be planted out in the open ground for the summer instead of being stood out in pots. They are lifted and brought into the greenhouse in September and this job will be made much easier if special planting baskets are used.

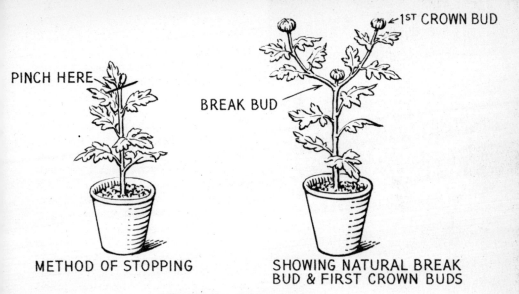

PINCH HERE

BREAK BUD

1ST CROWN BUD

METHOD OF STOPPING

SHOWING NATURAL BREAK
BUD & FIRST CROWN BUDS

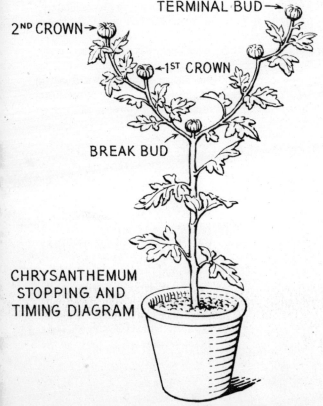

TERMINAL BUD →

2ND CROWN →

←1ST CROWN

BREAK BUD

CHRYSANTHEMUM
STOPPING AND
TIMING DIAGRAM

STOPPING

When the stem of a plant growing naturally reaches a certain height it develops a flower bud, called a break bud. This prevents any further extension of the stem and as the bud does not develop to flowering stage so early in the season the plant 'breaks' or produces new growths from the leaf axils below. These growths extend until they too produce flower buds known as First Crown Buds. If these buds are starved by the growths below or removed, another break occurs and the new stems produce Second Crown Buds. Occasionally further growths are required, to produce Terminal Buds.

In order to produce flowers earlier or to produce the best exhibition blooms and also to increase the number of flowers it is necessary to stop the plant artificially by pinching out the small growing point at the top of the stem.

Some plants do not need to be stopped as they produce their best blooms on a natural first crown or natural second crown. Others give their best blooms if stopped once, some have to be stopped twice.

The raiser of the variety usually determines which is the best bud to aim for and when to stop and states this in his catalogue, but the grower may find that local conditions affect this somewhat and is advised to make careful notes of the behaviour of his plants. Again, the date of rooting the cutting affects the stopping date appreciably. Most good nurserymen's catalogues give stopping dates and whether to aim for first or second crown buds.

The two upper pictures on the left show the growing tip being removed while in the lower picture the side growths have started to develop after the shoot has been removed.

Stopping dates for indoor varieties may vary between early April and mid-June while outdoor plants are usually stopped between mid-May and mid-June, according to variety.

In the top photograph on the left the plant has been stopped once and two laterals (side growths) have been allowed to develop. These are now being stopped in turn, in order to produce second crown buds. After this stopping new laterals will grow rapidly and eventually buds will be formed. The next operation is known as 'disbudding' or 'taking the bud' which means removing all unwanted buds leaving one only to flower on each stem (usually the centre one). In the top illustration on the right the tiny unwanted buds are being removed at an early stage. For exhibition plants of indoor varieties this is best done gradually over several days, removing the unwanted buds and side growths when about an inch long. (See below.)

If a bud seems to be developing too early for a particular show its flowering may be delayed by as much as ten days by delaying the removal of the surplus shoots. These may be left to reach a length of two or three inches before being removed. Care must be taken, however, not to starve the main bud by keeping the side shoots on too long.

About this time large numbers of side shoots will appear all over the plant and from the stool. These should all be removed. The plant above has developed large numbers of side growths and these have been removed in the illustration below.

By now the plant will be pot-bound and will need lots of water.

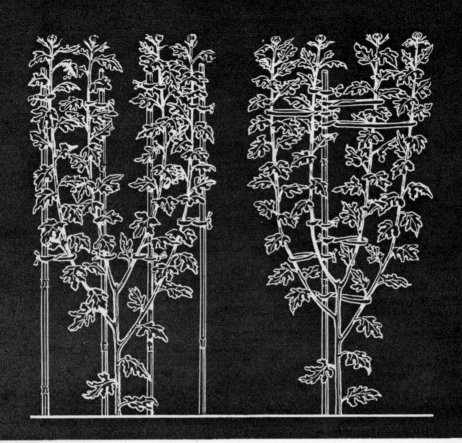

It is important to ensure that plants are properly staked and tied or high winds will cause untold damage. The drawing above shows methods of staking outdoor plants, using either four canes or a single cane. Four canes provide better support for the main growths can each have a cane.

The drawing below shows another method of delaying blooms for exhibition. If the chosen bud is developing too quickly it can be pinched out and a side shoot below allowed to grow on. This is called 'running on'.

The Cascade type of chrysanthemum which has been developed in recent years, can, as its name implies, be trained to produce a cascade of bloom. By careful pinching and stopping, and training the main stem downwards and towards the north the plant can be induced to develop scores of flowering shoots bearing hundreds of small flowers.

The plant above is being held up to show how the growths are tied to a length of wire netting in order to spread them out. Good plants will ultimately reach a length of 6 feet or more.

The illustration below shows how by careful feeding, training and dis-budding a specimen plant bearing fifteen or twenty blooms can be produced. Normally, exhibition plants are restricted to three or four stems, other plants to six or eight.

SHADING OUTDOOR BLOOMS

Blooms of outdoor varieties required for exhibition purposes require to be shaded from scorching sun and protected from rain and, in some parts of the country, from soot. There are several ways of doing this. Above, an erection suitable for an amateur growing a few plants is shown. The roofing material can be roofing felt, hessian or similar material. Note that plenty of air can circulate round the plants.

Below, a more ambitious erection is shown, suitable for the amateur who grows a large number of plants or for the professional grower. The light metal tubing used here is known as 'Klee-Clamp' and is both quick and easy to erect.

Individual blooms can be protected by placing paper cones over them or by putting the bud in a paper bag blown up and then tied tightly below the bud. Using the latter method blooms open cleanly and to their maximum size. The buds should be perfectly dry before placing the bag in position. The bloom is fully developed in two to three weeks after the bag is put on. Unless the weather is inclement the bag should be taken off about a day before cutting to allow the bloom to assume its natural shape. Blooms should be allowed to stand in water for a day before packing for the show.

HOUSING INDOOR VARIETIES

Late varieties planted out in the open ground should be lifted and planted in the greenhouse in September and plants in pots should also be brought inside. A1 and A2 above show plants which were planted out in wire baskets thus making for easier lifting. Plants not in baskets should be prepared for lifting about a week beforehand by cutting round them with a spade about 6 inches from the stem. Spreading roots will be severed but new fibrous ones will be encouraged. When lifted, as much soil as possible should be retained as shown at B. When housing carry in the plants pots first to avoid damage and arrange them on the staging in order of size, tallest at the back.

Above, left, a plant is being taken into the greenhouse pot first. The greenhouse should be properly cleaned and fumigated first, and the heating system checked over. Continue individual watering and ventilate freely, except during frost. About mid-October some heat may be needed, but only just enough to maintain the temperature at about 50°F. Fumigate regularly with BHC or DDT smokes. Remove and burn faded leaves. A modified feeding plan may be continued but it is better to give a final top dressing before housing and then only give clear water. Above, right, are first and second crown buds showing difference in time of development. Below

are well-balanced crown buds showing colour and about to open.

After the buds show colour no more feeding or fumigation should be carried out and care must be taken to see that all moisture has disappeared before ventilation is reduced at night.

CUTTING BLOOMS

When blooms are ready for cutting there are one or two hints worth noting. Never cut flowers from plants which are dry at the roots. Water well the day before. Cut the blooms so that they may stand in deep containers of water in a cool place for twelve hours before being packed. Always use a sharp knife and cut with an upward slanting movement. If correct cultivation has been carried out the stems of early flowering varieties should be pliable and soft. Those of indoor varieties are usually harder and in any case it is best to hammer their ends before putting them in deep water so that the maximum amount of water can be taken up.

TRANSPORTING BLOOMS

For transporting blooms to a show a deep, long box is first lined with soft paper. The blooms are then laid down on 'pillows' of soft paper rolled as shown and placed at both ends of the box just below the heads of the blooms. To accommodate a second layer of blooms further pillows are placed on top of and just below the heads of the blooms. The stems of the blooms are carefully pushed between those on the other side. Finally a piece of cane is wedged firmly across the box, a sheet of soft paper is placed over the blooms, and the lid of the box put on.

Those who have to travel long distances to shows or who have large blooms to carry can construct a hurdle box as illustrated on this page. It is 4 ft. long, 2 ft. 8 in. wide and 3 ft. high. Alternate short and long hurdles, $4\frac{1}{2}$ in. apart slide into grooves on the sides of the box. The lid is hinged and can be fastened with a hasp and staple.

Foliage is stripped off the stems of Large Exhibition blooms and a wire with a 3-inch ring is tied on to the stem below the calyx of those types with drooping flowers. The blooms are tied on to the hurdles and lowered into the box. To prevent bruising of petals a piece of soft tissue paper is tied between each bloom, and a zinc tube containing water is tied to the base of each stem. The main thing is to prevent the blooms from touching each other in transit.

49

On the left a hurdle box full of Large Exhibition blooms is shown. Note the wires on the stems, and the water containers. It can be seen how the use of alternate tall and short hurdles enables blooms with short stems to be carried below those with long stems.

Below is a close-up of the wire and ring used to support large recurving blooms. Large Exhibition blooms, their own stems having been stripped of leaves, usually have foliage stems wired on for exhibition purposes, as shown in the drawing. This is usually done on arrival at the show.

STAGING BLOOMS

Before staging the blooms each one should be examined to rectify any faults.   Faded, discoloured or damaged petals can be pulled out gently with tweezers.   An occasional petal which has become rolled or twisted can be straightened by gently rolling it over the finger with a pencil taking care not to bruise it.   Vases should be packed with rushes, privet stems or similar material to hold the stems steady.   Below, on the right, is a vase of three Large Exhibition blooms being staged to the best advantage.   Judges will look for freshness, colour, contour or shape, size (according to variety), perfect centres, quality and crispness of petal.   Name each flower legibly.

Above is a first prizewinning entry for a class of 18 large blooms staged at a National show. In this and the prizewinning entry below note the even quality of the blooms, the way in which they are staged to their best advantage. It is well worth while taking plenty of time over the staging of an exhibit. Place deep blooms at the back to make the best use of their depth. Shallower blooms placed in the front and lower, show greater width but their lack of depth tends to be hidden.

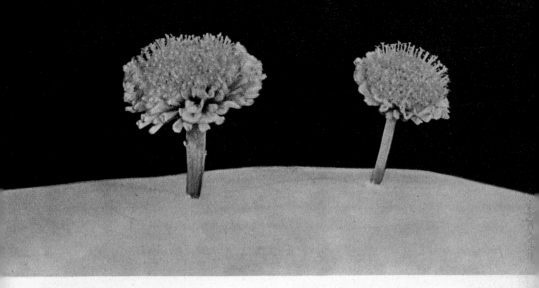

RAISING NEW VARIETIES

Keen amateurs may like to attempt the raising of new varieties from seed. Controlled crossings of selected varieties can be made in September. The plants used are raised from cuttings taken in January, their growth restricted by semi-starving them and stopping them two or three times to produce many laterals bearing single flowers with few petals (although grown normally the type may be double). From June onwards the plants should be in complete darkness each day from about 5 p.m. until 8 a.m. to encourage bud production.

Pollination consists in transferring ripe pollen from the anthers of one flower to the stigmas of another, using a camel hair brush. The petals are first closely trimmed as shown above to make the stigmas accessible.

On the right the various organs of the flower are shown.

An account such as this is necessarily incomplete and those interested are recommended to refer to a more complete work on the subject.

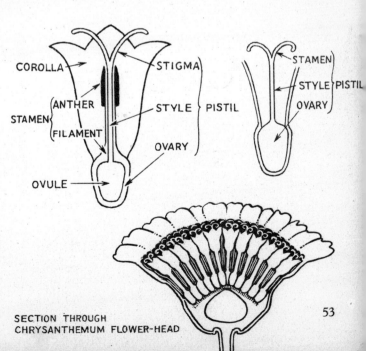

SECTION THROUGH
CHRYSANTHEMUM FLOWER-HEAD

53

| Capsid bug | Earwig damage | Leaf Miner damage |

PESTS AND DISEASES

Cleanliness at all stages is the first line of defence against pests and diseases. Regular spraying outside and fumigation in the greenhouse will deal with most pests and diseases.

DDT either alone or mixed with nicotine will kill capsid bugs and earwigs, while routine sprays with gamma-BHC will control the attacks of leaf miners.

On the left can be seen the effect of mineral deficiencies. The left-hand plant is healthy, that in the centre shows lack of magnesium (yellow patches between the leaf veins), and that on the right shows severe calcium deficiency (dieback from the tips of the shoots). To supply magnesium feed with Epsom salts at a teaspoonful per plant or spray with a solution of $\frac{1}{4}$ lb. of Epsom Salts in 2 gallons of water. Nothing can be done to save the right-hand plant, but earlier treatment is to add lime to cure the deficiency.

Damage and galls both caused by chrysanthemum midge   Eelworm damage

Symptoms of eelworm attack are triangular brownish patches between the veins of leaves which later turn black and droop against the stems before dropping off. Collect and burn all infected plant material and treat the stools by immersing them for 5 minutes in water at a constant temperature of 115°F.

DDT will control midge and thrips; nicotine, HETP, gamma-BHC will control aphis. Sulphur applied as a wettable spray or dust will control rust and mildew. Plants attacked by the bacterial disease leafy gall should be burnt, together with the soil they have grown in.

Rust   Mildew   Leafy gall disease

55

Progress, a typical pale pink medium-flowered Exhibition Incurved variety. *Cossack*, a Large Exhibition or Japanese variety. Red.

SOME TYPES OF CHRYSANTHEMUM

In the National Chrysanthemum Society's classification there are eleven sections for Indoor types, two for October flowering varieties and five for outdoor varieties.

The pinky mauve Large Exhibition Incurving variety *Shirley Triumph*. *Winn Quinn* is a typical Medium Exhibition variety ; yellow.

Lilac Loveliness, lilac-pink, is an excellent Reflexed Decorative. *Friendly Rival*, a popular late Incurving Decorative ; yellow.

On these and the following pages varieties representative of some of these types are shown. A good nurseryman's catalogue will list many beautiful varieties, while a visit to a show will enable the beginner to make a selection.

The pink and yellow Anemone-centred variety *Frieda*. *Little Dorrit* is a well-known outdoor Pompon ; pink.

Peter Robinson, a large-flowered Single variety; yellow. *Rayonnante* is a lilac-pink variety with extremely narrow, fluted petals.

On the facing page at the top is a typical *Charm* chrysanthemum bearing hundreds of small blooms. Below this is one of the recently introduced Lilliput types, *Happy*, clear yellow, blooming September to October.

Salmon Daydream is one of a popular family of outdoor Reflexed varieties. *John Woolman* is a recent pink addition to the outdoor Incurved varieties.

Above is a typical Korean variety *Venus*. Koreans, with their colourful single flowers, are easily grown and are excellent for cutting for decorative purposes.

On the left is another example of a Cascade chrysanthemum, *Yellow Spray*, with its many narrow-petalled starry flowers. Note the wire netting used for training and supporting the head of the plant.